Piano • Vocal • Guitar

Swinging Love

49 Romantic Swing Classics

ISBN 0-7935-9294-1

HAL•LEONARD®
CORPORATION

7777 W. BLUEMOUND RD. P.O. BOX 13819 MILWAUKEE, WI 53213

Visit Hal Leonard Online at
www.halleonard.com

Swinging Love

Contents

4	All of Me
8	The Blue Room
13	Blue Skies
18	Body and Soul
23	Can't Help Lovin' Dat Man
26	Candy
32	Cheek to Cheek
38	Come Rain or Come Shine
29	Day by Day
40	Dearly Beloved
46	Don't Get Around Much Anymore
43	Dream a Little Dream of Me
50	East of the Sun
58	Georgia on My Mind
53	Green Eyes
62	I Can't Give You Anything But Love
65	I'm Beginning to See the Light
68	I've Got My Love to Keep Me Warm
72	I've Got You Under My Skin
82	If I Were a Bell
77	Isn't It Romantic?
84	It's Only a Paper Moon

90	**Just in Time**
87	**Lazy River**
96	**Let There Be Love**
98	**Let's Fall in Love**
93	**L-O-V-E**
102	**Love Is a Simple Thing**
104	**Love Is Just Around the Corner**
108	**Makin' Whoopee!**
112	**My Baby Just Cares for Me**
116	**My Heart Stood Still**
120	**My Romance**
124	**Nevertheless**
127	**A Nightingale Sang in Berkeley Square**
132	**On a Slow Boat to China**
138	**One Dozen Roses**
142	**Our Day Will Come**
144	**Our Language of Love**
146	**Side by Side**
135	**There's a Small Hotel**
150	**This Can't Be Love**
152	**The Way You Look Tonight**
155	**Will You Still Be Mine**
163	**Witchcraft**
158	**You Brought a New Kind of Love to Me**
166	**You Made Me Love You**
170	**You'd Be So Nice to Come Home To**
173	**You're Nobody 'Til Somebody Loves You**

All of Me

Words and Music by SEYMOUR SIMONS
and GERALD MARKS

Lyrics:
You took my kiss-es and you took my love,— You taught me how to care; Am I to be— just the rem-nant of— a

I'm jealous of the moon that shines above
Because it smiles upon the ones I love
I'm jealous of the birdies in the trees
They alway singing sweetest melodies
I'm jealous of the pretty flowers too

I miss the kiss they always get from you
I'm jealous of the tick tock on the shelf
I'm even getting jealous of myself

The Blue Room
from THE GIRL FRIEND

Words by LORENZ HART
Music by RICHARD RODGERS

All my fu-ture plans, Dear, will suit your plans, Read the lit - tle blue prints; Here's your moth - er's room, Here's your

grand for us, Where we two can be our - selves, dear,

Slowly, with expression

We'll have a blue room, a new room, For

two room, Where ev - 'ry day's a hol - i - day Be -

cause you're mar - ried to me. Not like a

Blue Skies
from BETSY

Words and Music by
IRVING BERLIN

Body and Soul

Words by EDWARD HEYMAN,
ROBERT SOUR and FRANK EYTON
Music by JOHN GREEN

Can't Help Lovin' Dat Man

from SHOW BOAT

Lyrics by OSCAR HAMMERSTEIN II
Music by JEROME KERN

Candy

Words and Music by MACK DAVID,
JOAN WHITNEY and ALEX KRAMER

"Can - dy," I call my sug - ar

"Can - dy" be-cause I'm sweet on "Can - dy"

and "Can - dy's" sweet on me. {He} {She} un - der-

Day by Day

Theme from the Paramount Television Series DAY BY DAY

Words and Music by SAMMY CAHN,
AXEL STORDAHL and PAUL WESTON

Cheek to Cheek
from the RKO Radio Motion Picture TOP HAT

Words and Music by
IRVING BERLIN

Heav - en, _____ I'm in Heav - en. _____

And my heart beats so that I can hard - ly speak. _____

Come Rain or Come Shine
from ST. LOUIS WOMAN

Words by JOHNNY MERCER
Music by HAROLD ARLEN

Dearly Beloved
from YOU WERE NEVER LOVELIER

Music by JEROME KERN
Words by JOHNNY MERCER

Freely

Tell me that its true, _____ tell me you a - gree, _____

I was meant for you, _____ you were meant for

me. _____

Moderately

Dear - ly be - lov - ed, how

Dream a Little Dream of Me

Words by GUS KAHN
Music by WILBUR SCHWANDT and FABIAN ANDREE

Stars shin-ing bright a-bove you,

Night breez-es seem to whis-per, "I love you," Birds sing-ing in the

syc-a-more tree, "Dream a lit-tle dream of me."

Don't Get Around Much Anymore

Words and Music by BOB RUSSELL
and DUKE ELLINGTON

East of the Sun
(And West of the Moon)

Words and Music by
BROOKS BOWMAN

Green Eyes
(Aquellos Ojos Verdes)

Words and Music by ADOLFO UTRERA
and NILO MENDEZ

Life held no charm, dear, un-til I met you. _____
Fue - ron tus o - jos los que me die - rón _____

Georgia on My Mind

Words by STUART GORRELL
Music by HOAGY CARMICHAEL

I Can't Give You Anything But Love

from BLACKBIRDS OF 1928

Words by DOROTHY FIELDS
Music by JIMMY McHUGH

I'm Beginning to See the Light

Words and Music by DON GEORGE, JOHNNY HODGES,
DUKE ELLINGTON and HARRY JAMES

I've Got My Love to Keep Me Warm

from the 20th Century Fox Motion Picture ON THE AVENUE

Words and Music by
IRVING BERLIN

I've Got You Under My Skin

from BORN TO DANCE

Words and Music by
COLE PORTER

Isn't It Romantic?

from the Paramount Picture LOVE ME TONIGHT

Words by LORENZ HART
Music by RICHARD RODGERS

Calmly

mp

Ab Abm Eb Bb7

Fm7 Bb7 Ab Abm

I've nev - er met you, yet nev - er
My face is glow - ing, I'm en - er -

Eb/G Gbdim Fm7 Bb7#5

doubt, dear, I can't for - get you, I've thought you
get - ic, the art of sew - ing, I found po -

Ebmaj7 Ab Bb7

out, dear. I know your pro - file and I know the way you
et - ic. My nee - dle punc - tu - ates the rhy - thm of ro -

If I Were a Bell
from GUYS AND DOLLS

By FRANK LOESSER

It's Only a Paper Moon

featured in the Motion Picture PAPER MOON

Lyric by BILLY ROSE and E.Y. HARBURG
Music by HAROLD ARLEN

Lazy River

Words and Music by HOAGY CARMICHAEL
and SIDNEY ARODIN

Just in Time
from BELLS ARE RINGING

Words by BETTY COMDEN and ADOLPH GREEN
Music by JULE STYNE

L-O-V-E

Words and Music by BERT KAEMPFERT
and MILT GABLER

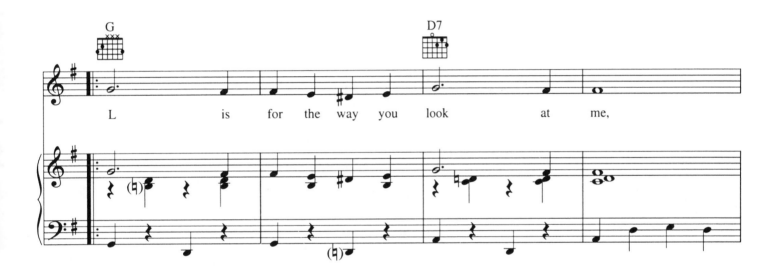

Let There Be Love

Lyric by IAN GRANT
Music by LIONEL RAND

Let's Fall in Love

Words by TED KOEHLER
Music by HAROLD ARLEN

Love Is a Simple Thing

Words by JUNE CARROLL
Music by ARTHUR SIEGEL

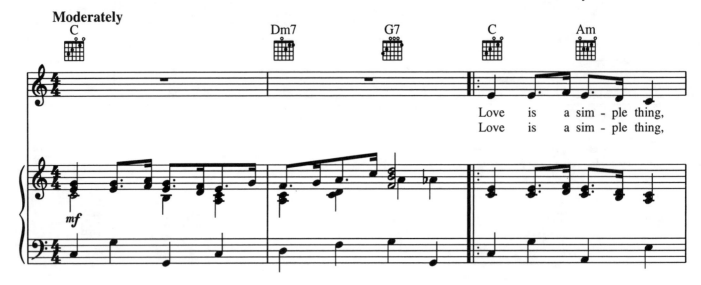

Love is a sim - ple thing,
Love is a sim - ple thing,

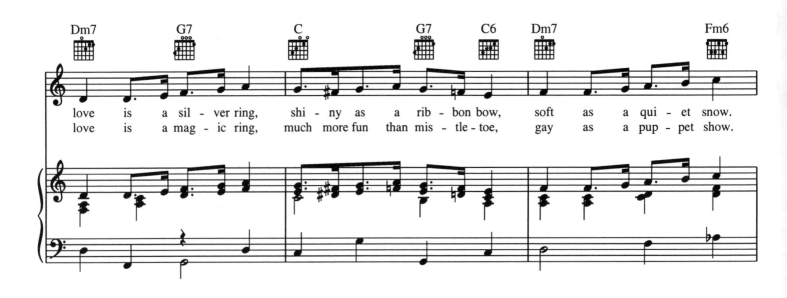

love is a sil - ver ring, shi - ny as a rib - bon bow, soft as a qui - et snow.
love is a mag - ic ring, much more fun than mis - tle - toe, gay as a pup - pet show.

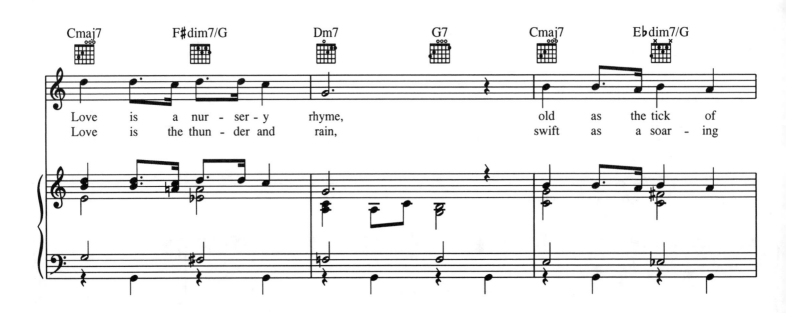

Love is a nur - ser - y rhyme, old as the tick of
Love is the thun - der and rain, swift as a soar - ing

Love Is Just Around the Corner

from the Paramount Picture HERE IS MY HEART

Words and Music by LEO ROBIN
and LEWIS E. GENSLER

Makin' Whoopee!
from WHOOPEE!

Lyrics by GUS KAHN
Music by WALTER DONALDSON

110

My Baby Just Cares for Me

Lyrics by GUS KAHN
Music by WALTER DONALDSON

I'm so hap-py since the day___ I
fell in love___ in a great big way___ and the big sur-prise is

My Heart Stood Still

from ONE DAM THING AFTER ANOTHER

Words by LORENZ HART
Music by RICHARD RODGERS

My Romance
from JUMBO

Words by LORENZ HART
Music by RICHARD RODGERS

Nevertheless
(I'm in Love with You)

Words and Music by BERT KALMAR
and HARRY RUBY

A Nightingale Sang in Berkeley Square

Lyric by ERIC MASCHWITZ
Music by MANNING SHERWIN

*Pronounced "Bar-kley"

On a Slow Boat to China

By FRANK LOESSER

Slowly, with a beat

There's a Small Hotel

from ON YOUR TOES

Words by LORENZ HART
Music by RICHARD RODGERS

Lyrics:

There's a small ho-tel With a wish-ing well; I wish that we were there to-geth - er.

There's a brid - al suite; One room bright and neat, Com -

One Dozen Roses

Words by ROGER LEWIS and "COUNTRY" JOE WASHBURN
Music by DICK JURGENS and WALTER DONOVAN

Our Day Will Come

Words by BOB HILLIARD
Music by MORT GARSON

MCA Music Publishing

Our Language of Love

from IRMA LA DOUCE

Music by MARGUERITE MONNOT
Original French words by ALEXANDRE BREFFORT
English words by JULIAN MORE, DAVID HENEKER and MONTY NORMAN

Side by Side

Words and Music by
HARRY WOODS

This Can't Be Love
from THE BOYS FROM SYRACUSE

Words by LORENZ HART
Music by RICHARD RODGERS

The Way You Look Tonight

from SWING TIME

Words by DOROTHY FIELDS
Music by JEROME KERN

Will You Still Be Mine

Words by TOM ADAIR
Music by MATT DENNIS

You Brought a New Kind of Love to Me

from the Paramount Picture THE BIG POND

Words and Music by SAMMY FAIN,
IRVING KAHAL and PIERRE NORMAN

Witchcraft

Lyric by CAROLYN LEIGH
Music by CY COLEMAN

You Made Me Love You
(I Didn't Want to Do It)
from BROADWAY MELODY OF 1938

Words by JOE McCARTHY
Music by JAMES V. MONACO

You'd Be So Nice to Come Home To
from SOMETHING TO SHOUT ABOUT

Words and Music by
COLE PORTER

Rather Slow with Feeling

You'd be

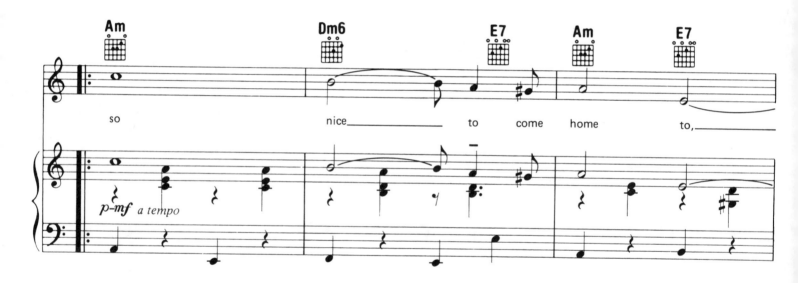

so   nice_____ to come home   to,_____

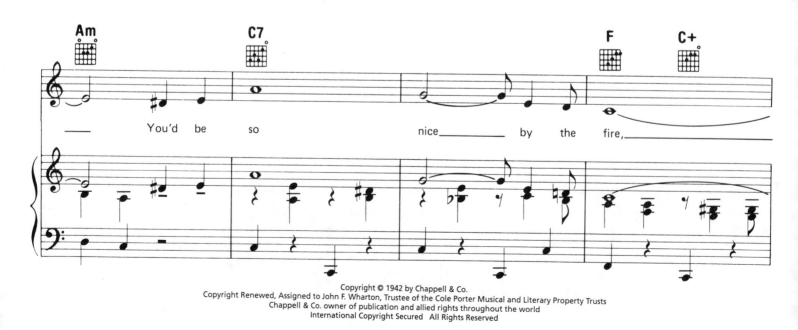

_____ You'd be so   nice_____ by the   fire,_____

You're Nobody 'Til Somebody Loves You

Words and Music by RUSS MORGAN,
LARRY STOCK and JAMES CAVANAUGH

Some look for glo-ry, it's still the old sto-ry of love ver-sus glo-ry, and when all is said and done: You're no-bod-y 'til some-bod-y loves you, _____ you're

Classic Collections Of Your Favorite Songs

arranged for piano, voice, and guitar.

Beautiful Ballads

A massive collection of 87 songs, including: April In Paris • Autumn In New York • Call Me Irresponsible • Cry Me A River • I Wish You Love • I'll Be Seeing You • If • Imagine • Isn't It Romantic? • It's Impossible (Somos Novios) • Mona Lisa • Moon River • People • The Way We Were • A Whole New World (Aladdin's Theme) • and more.
00311679 ....$17.95

The Big Book of Standards

86 classics essential to any music library, including: April In Paris • Autumn In New York • Blue Skies • Cheek To Cheek • Heart And Soul • I Left My Heart In San Francisco • In The Mood • Isn't It Romantic? • Mona Lisa • Moon River • The Nearness Of You • Out Of Nowhere • Spanish Eyes • Star Dust • Stella By Starlight • That Old Black Magic • They Say It's Wonderful • What Now My Love • and more.
00311667 ....$19.95

Remember This One?

43 classics, including: Ac-cent-tchu-ate The Positive • Ain't She Sweet • Autumn Leaves • (The Original) Boogie Woogie • A Good Man Is Hard To Find • I Wanna Be Loved By You • Mister Sandman • Sentimental Journey • Sioux City Sue • Unchained Melody • and more.
00384600 ....$12.95

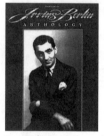

Irving Berlin Anthology

A comprehensive collection of 61 timeless songs with a bio, song background notes, and photos. Songs include: Always • Blue Skies • Cheek To Cheek • God Bless America • Marie • Puttin' On The Ritz • Steppin' Out With My Baby • There's No Business Like Show Business • White Christmas • (I Wonder Why?) You're Just In Love • and more.
00312493 ....$19.95

Classic Jazz Standards

56 jazz essentials: All the Things You Are • Don't Get Around Much Anymore • How Deep Is the Ocean • In the Wee Small Hours of the Morning • Polka Dots and Moonbeams • Satin Doll • Skylark • Tangerine • Tenderly • What's New? • and more.
00310310 ....$16.95

The Best of Rodgers & Hammerstein

A capsule of 26 classics from this legendary duo. Songs include: Climb Ev'ry Mountain • Edelweiss • Getting To Know You • I'm Gonna Wash That Man Right Outa My Hair • My Favorite Things • Oklahoma • The Surrey With The Fringe On Top • You'll Never Walk Alone • and more.
00308210 ....$12.95

The Best Standards Ever Volume 1 (A-L)

72 beautiful ballads, including: All The Things You Are • Bewitched • Can't Help Lovin' Dat Man • Don't Get Around Much Anymore • Getting To Know You • God Bless' The Child • Hello, Young Lovers • I Got It Bad And That Ain't Good • It's Only A Paper Moon • I've Got You Under My Skin • The Lady Is A Tramp • Little White Lies.
00359231 ....$15.95

I'll Be Seeing You: 50 Songs of World War II

A salute to the music and memories of WWII, including a year-by-year chronology of events on the homefront, dozens of photos, and 50 radio favorites of the GIs and their families back home, including: Boogie Woogie Bugle Boy • Don't Sit Under The Apple Tree (With Anyone Else But Me) • I Don't Want To Walk Without You • I'll Be Seeing You • Moonlight In Vermont • There's A Star-Spangled Banner Waving Somewhere • You'd Be So Nice To Come Home To • and more.
00311698 ....$19.95

The Best Songs Ever

80 must-own classics, including: All I Ask Of You • Body And Soul • Crazy • Endless Love • Fly Me To The Moon • Here's That Rainy Day • In The Mood • Love Me Tender • Memory • Moonlight In Vermont • My Funny Valentine • People • Satin Doll • Save The Best For Last • Somewhere Out There • Strangers In The Night • Tears In Heaven • A Time For Us • The Way We Were • When I Fall In Love • You Needed Me • and more.
00359224 .... $19.95

The Best Standards Ever Volume 2 (M-Z)

72 songs, including: Makin' Whoopee • Misty • Moonlight In Vermont • My Funny Valentine • Old Devil Moon • The Party's Over • People Will Say We're In Love • Smoke Gets In Your Eyes • Strangers In The Night • Tuxedo Junction • Yesterday.
00359232 ....$15.95

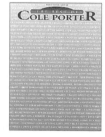

Best of Cole Porter

38 of his classics, including: All Of You • Anything Goes • Be A Clown • Don't Fence Me In • I Get A Kick Out Of You • In The Still Of The Night • Let's Do It (Let's Fall In Love) • Night And Day • You Do Something To Me • and many
00311577 ....$14.95

Torch Songs

Sing your heart out with this collection of 59 sultry jazz and big band melancholy masterpieces, including: Angel Eyes • Cry Me A River • I Can't Get Started • I Got It Bad And That Ain't Good • I'm Glad There Is You • Lover Man (Oh, Where Can You Be?) • Misty • My Funny Valentine • Stormy Weather • and many more! 224 pages.
00490446 ....$16.95